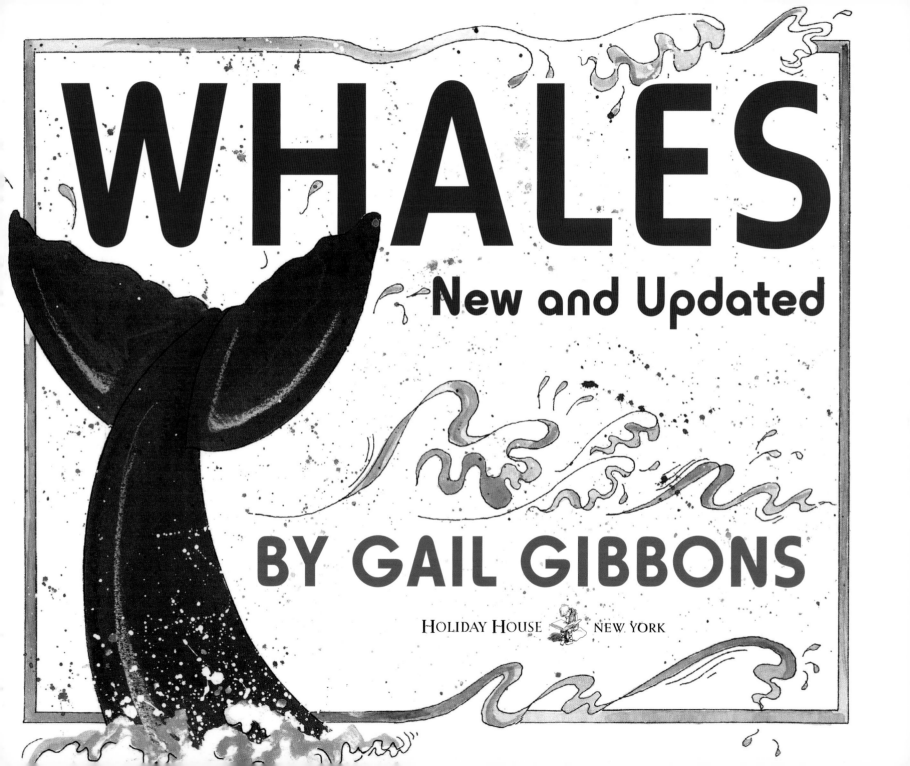

WHALES

New and Updated

BY GAIL GIBBONS

HOLIDAY HOUSE • NEW YORK

For Karen, Peter, and Kirsten Collins

Special thanks to Sara Ketelsen, Mammalogy Museum
Specialist of the American Museum of Natural History

Copyright © 1991, 2022 by Gail Gibbons
All Rights Reserved
HOLIDAY HOUSE is registered in the U.S. Patent and Trademark Office.
Printed and bound in January 2022 at Toppan Leefung, DongGuan, China.
Second Edition.
1 3 5 7 9 10 8 6 4 2

The Library of Congress has cataloged the previous edition as follows:
Gibbons, Gail.
Whales / by Gail Gibbons. — 1st ed.
p.   cm.
Summary: Introduces different kinds of whales.
ISBN 0-8234-0900-7
1. Whales—Juvenile literature. [1. Whales.] I. Title.
QL737.C4G37   1991   91-4507   CIP   AC
599.5—dc20

ISBN: 978-0-8234-5175-3 (revised hardcover)
ISBN: 978-0-8234-1030-9 (revised paperback)

Whales live in oceans. They are not fish. They are air-breathing, warm-blooded mammals.

Some are small, and others are huge!

The world's largest animals are whales.

MESONYCHID
mes·o·NICK·id

The first ancestors of whales lived more than 50 million years ago. Scientists believe they are descended from creatures that lived on land, possibly the mesonychid.

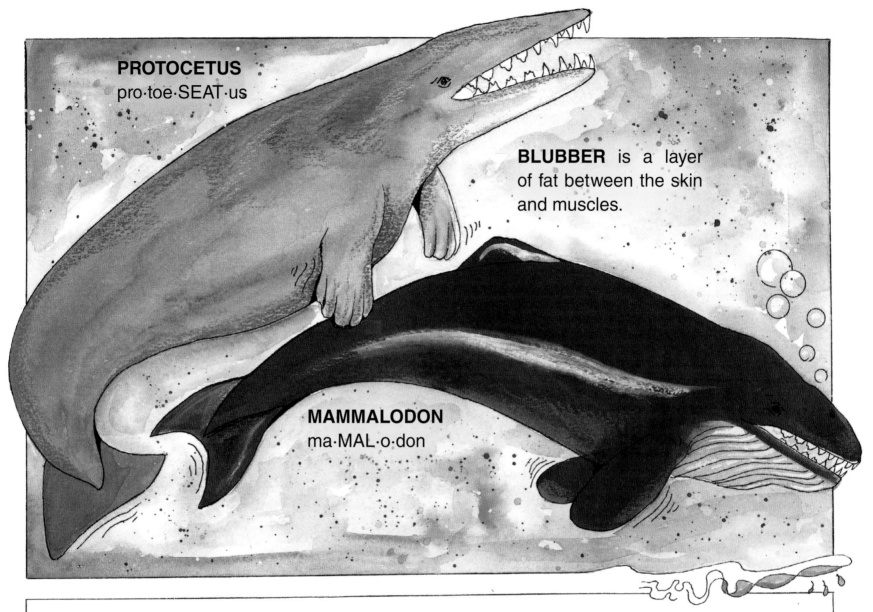

PROTOCETUS
pro·toe·SEAT·us

BLUBBER is a layer of fat between the skin and muscles.

MAMMALODON
ma·MAL·o·don

At some point, they began to stay in the oceans. Their bodies became more streamlined for easier swimming. Their fur was replaced by blubber to keep them warm.

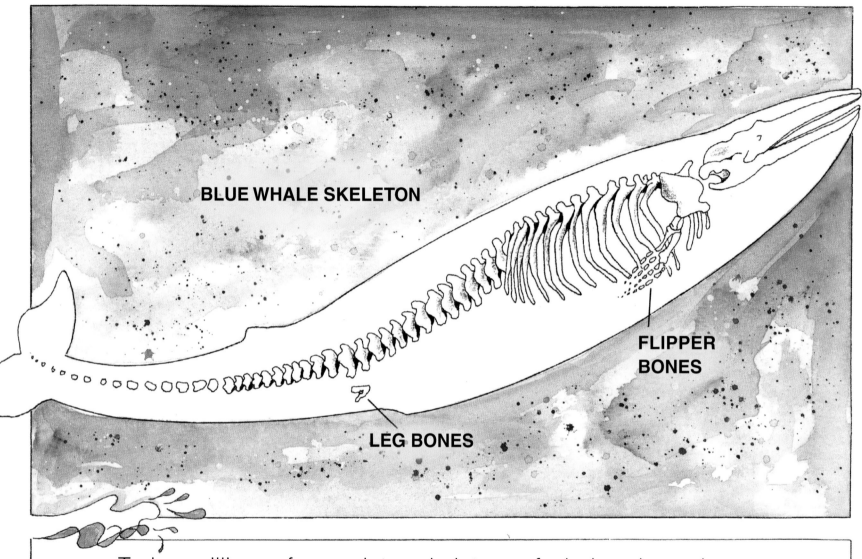

BLUE WHALE SKELETON

FLIPPER BONES

LEG BONES

Today, millions of years later, skeletons of whales show clues to their early ancestors. Inside their flippers are bones arranged like those of a hand. Further back there are remains of small leg bones, but there are no flippers here.

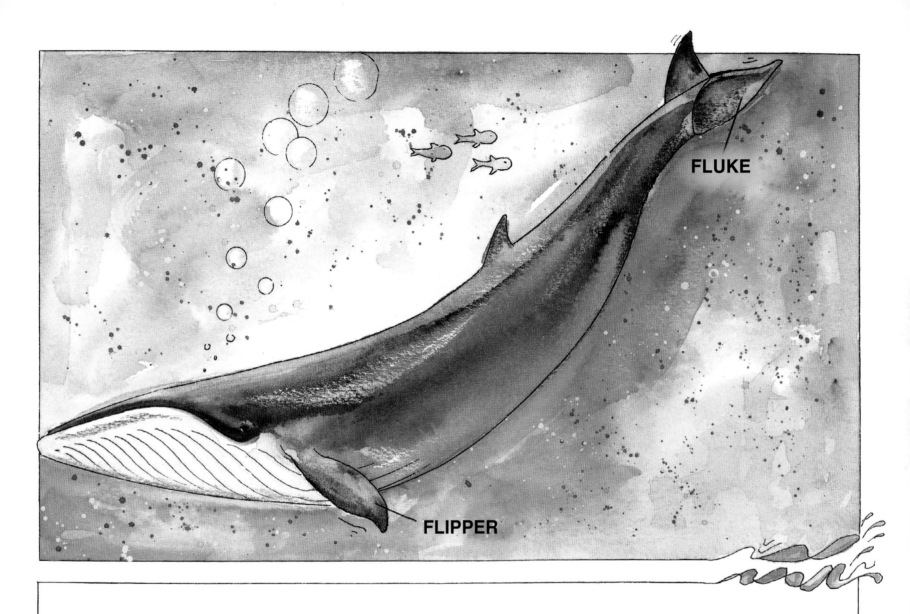

FLUKE

FLIPPER

Whales' tails are called flukes. They don't look like fish tails. Whales push themselves through the water by moving their flukes up and down. They use their flippers for balance and turning.

BLOWHOLE

Whales can't stay under water like fish. Beneath the surface they must hold their breath. Before diving, whales breathe fresh air into their lungs through one or two nostrils on top of their heads. They are called blowholes.

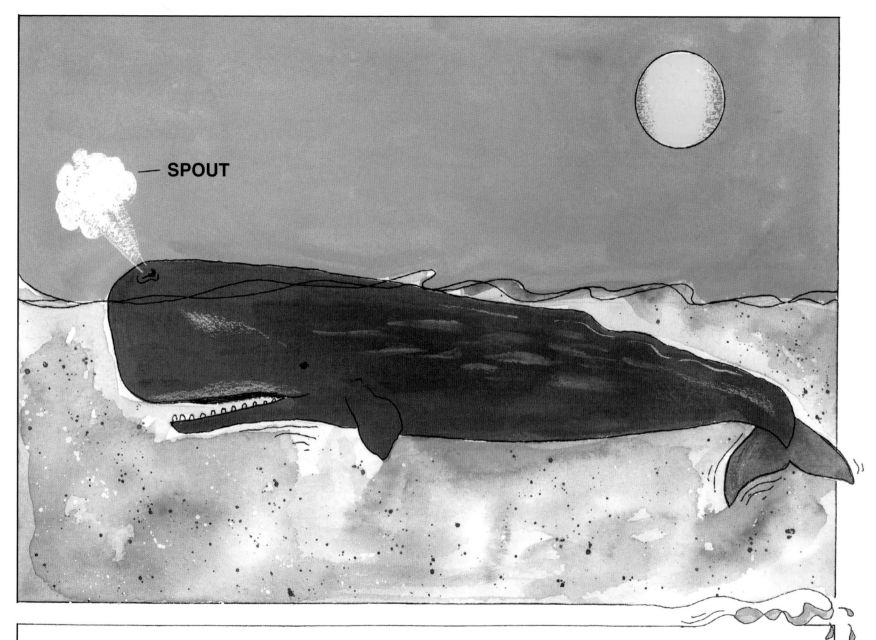

SPOUT

When whales surface, they blow out their wet, warm breath, making a spout.

SONAR or
ECHOLOCATION
ek·o·low·KAY·shun

When some whales can't see well in dark and murky waters, they make clicking sounds. The sound waves travel and bounce off objects. Then they come back to the whales' ears. This is called sonar or echolocation.

Some whales make other sounds, too. They resemble squeals, groans, chirps, and whistles like birds. Scientists believe that whales make these sounds to communicate with each other.

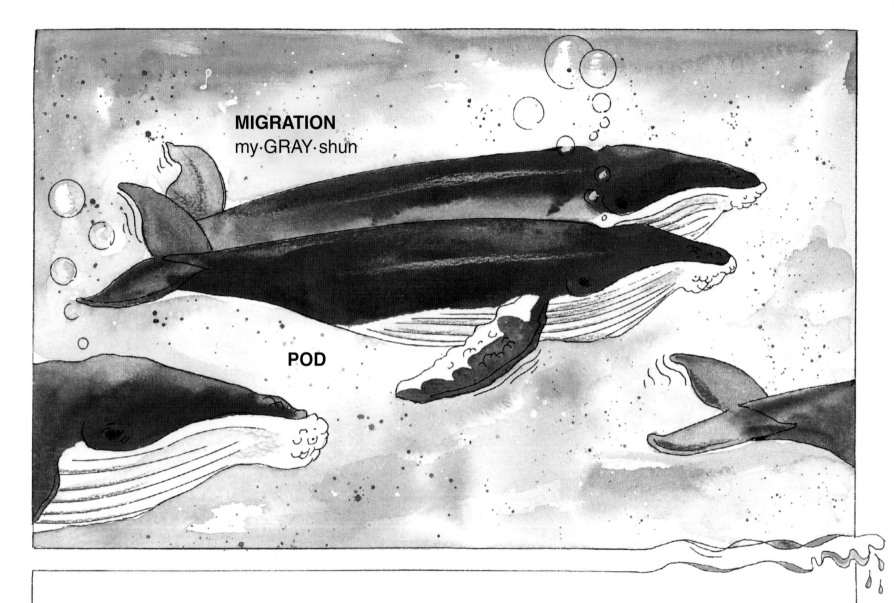

MIGRATION
my·GRAY·shun

POD

Some whales travel to cold waters to feed and live in the summer. Often they travel in groups, called pods. In the winter they go back to the warmer waters. This traveling is called migration.

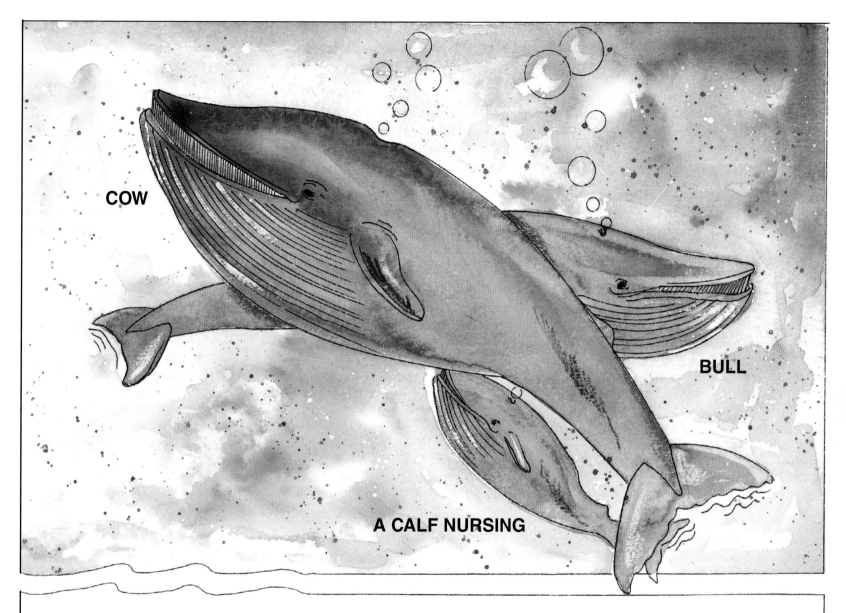

COW

BULL

A CALF NURSING

In the warm waters, the females have their babies. They can only have one baby at a time. A male is called a bull and a female is called a cow. A baby is called a calf.

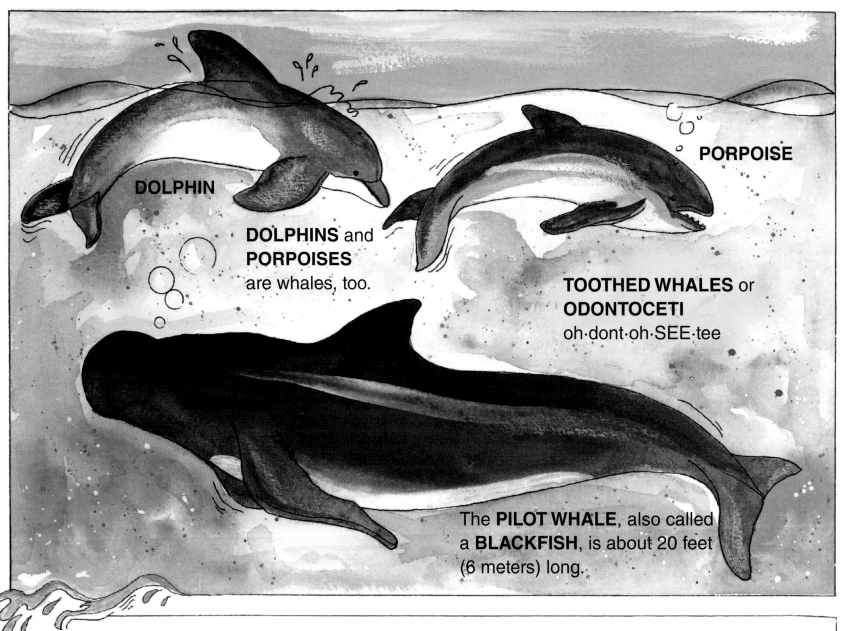

DOLPHIN

PORPOISE

DOLPHINS and
PORPOISES
are whales, too.

TOOTHED WHALES or
ODONTOCETI
oh·dont·oh·SEE·tee

The **PILOT WHALE**, also called
a **BLACKFISH**, is about 20 feet
(6 meters) long.

There are two main kinds of whales. One group has teeth.
They are called toothed whales, or Odontoceti.

The **NARWHAL** has two teeth. In the males, one of the teeth grows into a long tusk.

The **BELUGA** (bah·LOO·ga), also called a **WHITE WHALE**, lives near the North Pole. It is about 16 feet (5 meters) long.

Most toothed whale males are larger than the females.

A **SPERM WHALE** can stay under water for a very long time. It can be around 50 feet (15 meters) long.

Toothed whales have only one blowhole.

The **KILLER WHALE**, also called an **ORCA**, has sharp teeth. It eats fish, penguins, seals, and even some of the bigger whales! It can be about 30 feet (9 meters) long.

The teeth are only for catching their food.
They gulp down their food without chewing.

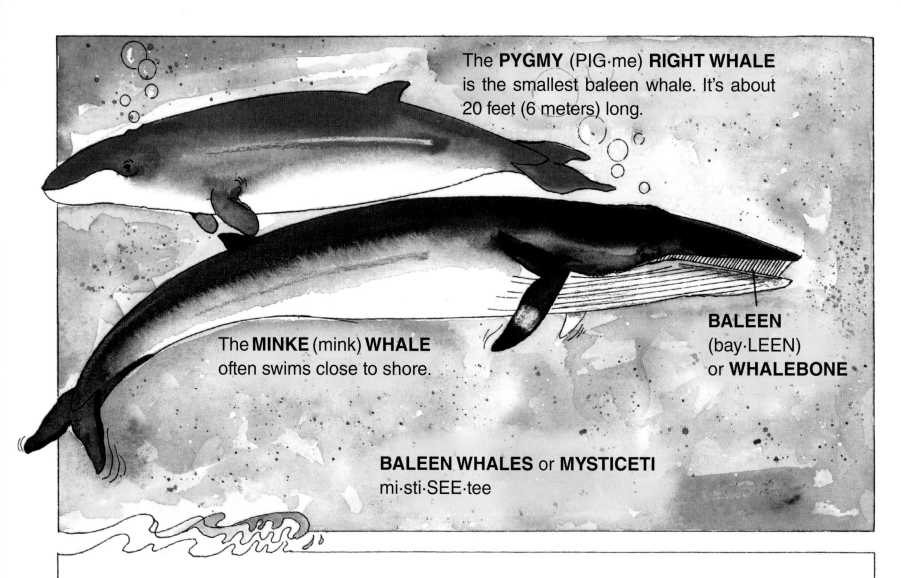

The **PYGMY** (PIG·me) **RIGHT WHALE** is the smallest baleen whale. It's about 20 feet (6 meters) long.

The **MINKE** (mink) **WHALE** often swims close to shore.

BALEEN (bay·LEEN) or **WHALEBONE**

BALEEN WHALES or **MYSTICETI** mi·sti·SEE·tee

The other main group of whales has no teeth. Instead, they have long, fringed blades hanging from their upper jaws that strain out their food from the water. The blades are called baleen, or whalebone. Baleen whales are also called Mysticeti.

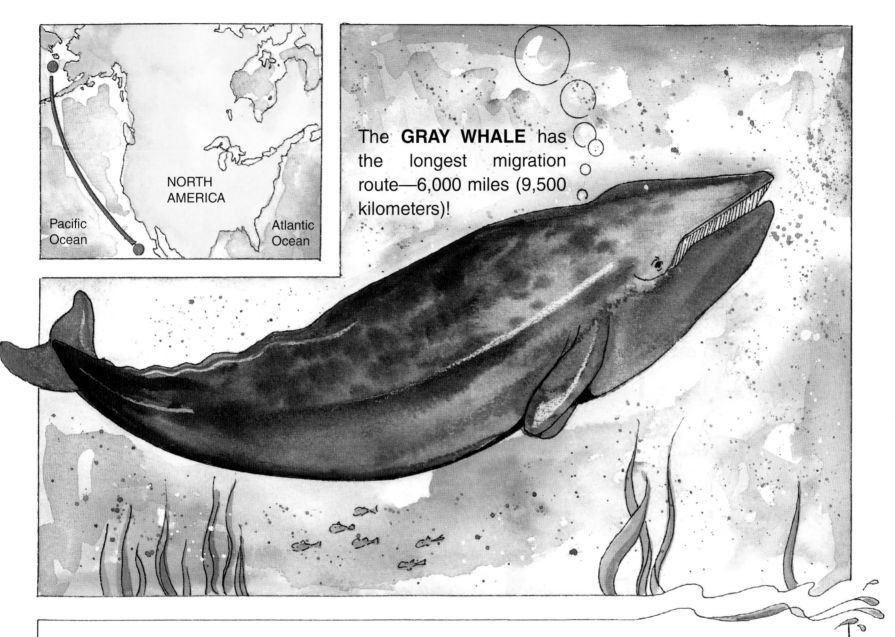

NORTH
AMERICA

Pacific
Ocean

Atlantic
Ocean

The **GRAY WHALE** has the longest migration route—6,000 miles (9,500 kilometers)!

Baleen whales eat fish and a mixture of tiny plants called plankton.
In the plankton are shrimplike creatures called krill.

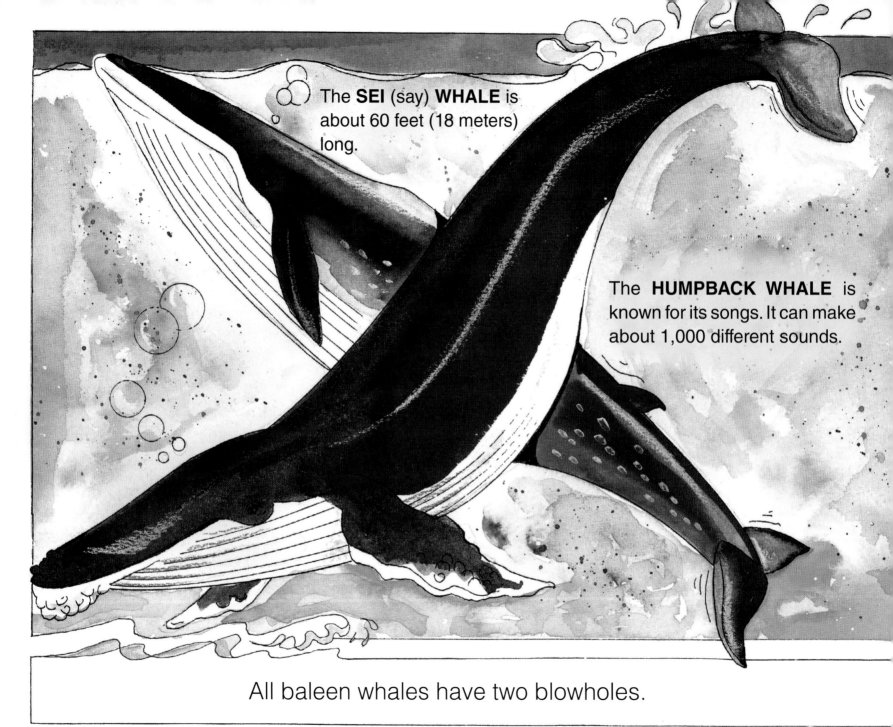

The **SEI** (say) **WHALE** is about 60 feet (18 meters) long.

The **HUMPBACK WHALE** is known for its songs. It can make about 1,000 different sounds.

All baleen whales have two blowholes.

The **RIGHT WHALE** has a huge head and is about 55 feet (17 meters) long.

The female baleen whales are often larger than the males.

The **BOWHEAD WHALE**, also called the **GREENLAND RIGHT WHALE**, has the longest baleen of any whale, around 15 feet (5 meters) long.

Baleen whales are among the biggest of the whales.

The **FIN WHALE** is huge. It got its name from the hooked fin on its back.

Some baleen whales have grooves on their skin from their chins to their bellies.

The **BLUE WHALE** is the biggest creature that ever lived, even bigger than the biggest dinosaur!

Baleen whales are graceful . . .

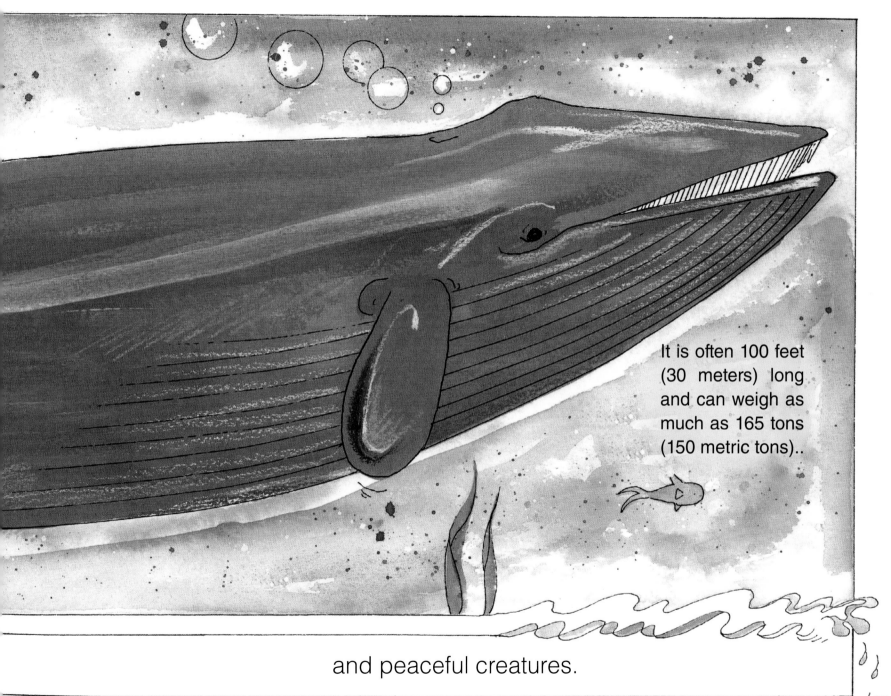

It is often 100 feet (30 meters) long and can weigh as much as 165 tons (150 metric tons)..

and peaceful creatures.

There used to be millions of whales in the oceans. For thousands of years they were hunted for their meat, hide, and bones. About 200 years ago, whalers began hunting them even more for other products.

They used different parts of whales to make lamp oil, soap, candles, and cosmetics. The whalers used the baleen to make buggy whips, umbrellas, and stiffening for clothes. Over the years, there were fewer and fewer whales.

Today, people are worried about how small the whale population has become. Some laws have been passed to protect them from being hunted. Sometimes people go on whale watches to see these creatures in their natural home, the ocean.

Scientists have learned that there are about 100 different kinds of whales. They are graceful and beautiful wonders of the sea.

WHALE TALES

In 1851, Herman Melville wrote a book called *Moby Dick*. One of the most famous books ever written, it told about a magnificent white sperm whale that whalers were hunting.

A blue whale eats about 8,000 pounds (3,500 kg) of krill a day.

Now and then whales accidentally swim onto a beach and become stranded. Sometimes, people help them return to the sea so they won't die.

A sperm whale can dive down more than a half mile.

A baby blue whale is the biggest baby in the world. At birth it is about 25 feet (8 meters) long and can weigh around 4,000 pounds (2,000 kg).

The Cuvier's beaked whale is the deepest diving mammal on earth. It can dive to about 10,000 feet (3,000 meters) and hold its breath for at least an hour.

Breaching is when a whale leaps from the water.

A blue whale is so big that 50 people could stand on its tongue.

In 1985, Humphrey the humpback whale became lost and wandered up California's Sacramento River. Scientists lured Humphrey back to sea by playing a tape of humpback whale songs.

In 1990, Humphrey was stranded in San Francisco Bay. Thousands of Humphrey fans watched scientists help him get back out to sea again.

Recorded sounds of humpback whales have been sent into outer space on *Voyager 1* and *2*.